I LIVE
REAL CLOSE
TO WHERE
YOU USED
TO LIVE

McSweeney's Books
San Francisco
www.mcsweeneys.net

Copyright © 2010 McSweeney's and 826 National

Cover design: Walter Green
Cover illustration: Renea Harris-Peterson
Design: Walter Green & Eliana Stein

Printed in the U.S.A.

ISBN 978-1-936365-20-3

I LIVE REAL CLOSE TO
WHERE YOU USED TO LIVE

Kids' Letters to Michelle Obama
(and to Sasha, Malia, and Bo)

EDITED BY LAUREN HALL

DURING HER FIRST TWO YEARS as the
First Lady, Michelle Obama has established a powerful legacy.
Her passions come through in her work with issues close to her
heart — helping women balance career and family, encouraging national service, promoting the arts, and advocating healthy
eating and healthy living for families across the country. But
she has also made it clear that before her role as a first lady, first
and foremost she is Malia and Sasha's mom. She has young
people on her mind, and she has worked tirelessly to reach
them, hear them, and to advocate for their well-being.

Shortly after Barack Obama's election in the fall of 2008, our
nonprofit writing and tutoring organization, 826 National,
asked students to write letters to our new president, putting
on paper the questions, advice, and special requests they
had brewing. As most of the students had only known one
presidency throughout their lives, this was an important
moment for them, and they were eager to participate.

We turned their heartfelt pieces into a collection called
*Thanks and Have Fun Running the Country: Kids' Letters to
President Obama*. When the book came out, our students read
their letters to packed audiences and signed autographs at

bookstores across the country. In January 2009, some of the pieces landed on the Op-Ed page of the *New York Times.* That spring, our most burning question was answered when we came across an *Associated Press* photo of President Obama holding that very edition of the *New York Times,* folded open to the page those pieces appeared on. He took some suggestions to heart and skipped others — he didn't, for example, put a snow cone in the hand of every American. He *did* focus on a health-care bill, as suggested by thirteen-year-old student Heaven Willis. We had the president's ear!

Now here we are, at the halfway point of Obama's presidential term, and this time around the students are offering their words of wisdom to the First Lady. We gave them the opportunity to send letters to Michelle, and they've responded with a vision for what their lives and their country might be like under the influence of a powerful, inspiring, and effective woman.

Within these pages we see Michelle Obama from the perspective of our young students. They are speaking to a woman they consider to be simultaneously maternal and cool. Not surprisingly, they give her points here for her eloquent speeches and her tireless work for children. But they also address tough ongoing issues — childhood obesity, the wars, poorly funded schools — and get personal, telling stories about their families and their most embarrassing moments. And in an interesting departure from the first collection, here the students pay particular attention to their subject's dance moves and keen fashion sense. The topics are broad, but the kids have faith that Michelle is their advocate and that she is listening.

Throughout, it's especially clear that Michelle Obama's passions have resonated with these young people, and that they trust her. The letters are candid and sincere — "What if I was your daughter?" "Could you help me in my quest to promote sustainable fashion?" "You are the best wife of a president. I am ordinary. You are the wife of President Obama." It's as though the students can imagine strolling on the White House lawn, playing in the garden, and eating macaroni and cheese with Michelle and her family. They share their plans with her, and they ask her for her help.

So once again, we present a delightful blend of poignant, quirky, and simply brilliant ideas straight from the surprising minds of young people. There's a lot to consider in these pages, and some pretty tall orders. It's a worthy exercise to wonder how our lives would be in a world of the students' creation: everything costs a dollar, no animals are endangered, and everyone's father has a job. We hope Michelle will enjoy diving in as much as we did. She has her homework cut out for her, but if she'll heed eight-year-old Laurea's advice — "Do what you can and it will be perfect" — she should be in good shape.

Lauren Hall, Editor
November 2010

Mildred Dzib, age 10, San Francisco

"You're a better dancer than your husband."

Dear Mrs. Obama,

You're the greatest person I ever met. I know that you married Obama because he cares about people and also you think he is a special person. You make great speeches. I really know that you have a great family. How big is your garden? I hope you have great vegetables and fruits so your two children can be strong and grow, too. You're a better dancer than your husband.

I live in Los Angeles. I live in a white and gray apartment. I watch videos. I'm a girl who is ten years old. My favorite things are soccer, movies, and also princesses. Do you think princesses are for little kids? My favorite fruit is mango. What is your favorite fruit? My parents are very nice. I really want letters from your whole family at the White House. When I grow up I want to help persons just like you.

Love,
Tatiana Morales, age 10
Los Angeles

"I am writing to you proposing that you could help me in my quest to promote sustainable fashion."

Dear First Lady,

Something that is very important to me is sustainability and the use of organic materials in fashion. To me, the fact that I can take an old T-shirt and turn it into thirty bracelets proves that my possibilities for fashionable opportunities to help the world are endless.

As first lady, you have become widely known as a fashion icon around the world. Women see you as an empowering female figure helping to make our world a better place, and naturally want to make themselves more like you. So I am writing to you proposing that you could help me in my quest to promote sustainable fashion.

People say the best outfits are the ones that make statements, and it seems to me that the idea of making organic, sustainable choices is a statement you would be perfect for making, not only with your clothing but with that of your daughters.

I understand if you can't, but I would greatly appreciate any help you can give in making the fashion world a little more eco-friendly.

Thank you so much,
Lucille Corbit, age 14
Seattle

"Can I have $10,000 to buy my passport to go to Las Vegas?"

Dear Michelle,

Can I borrow some money so we can move into an apartment and buy a new Mustang convertible? I don't mean to waste money. I will use some of the money to buy a drum set and have a cool pool. Can I have $10,000 to buy my passport to go to Las Vegas? Send me a picture of the White House and the statue of Abraham Lincoln.

Love,
Luis Molina, age 10
Los Angeles

Dear First Lady Michelle Obama,

My parents are divorced. I am having trouble moving on. Do you have any tips? I am confused and sad.

Your admirer,
Mai Robinson, age 9
Los Angeles

Dear Obama family,

I am going to be in the second grade. Do you get a lot of
threats? I have nine rooms in my house. I would like to be
the first woman to become president. Do you like dogs and
hamsters? Do you guys have a lot of allergies? Do you like
pizza, popcorn, and ice cream? What school do you go to?
I go to McDade Classical School. I like to play and ride my
bike. Our dads know each other.

Your friend,
Mikaela J.L. Ewing, age 7
Chicago

826 Seattle
8414 Greenwood Ave. n.
Seattle WA 98103

August 11, 2010

White house
1600 Pennsylvania Ave. NW
washinton DC 20500

Dear First lady,
my name is Hank
I am 8 years old.
I have created a holiday you
may like. The holiday is nathonol
read day! People alllll over the
country would read to themselves
and others. I think you should try
ate have people celebrate it.

sincerely,
Hank

P.S. it is on Dec. 15
P.P.S. that is my Birthday

Hank Fialko, age 8, Seattle

Dear Michelle Obama,

You are a nice lady. I don't like pepperoni pizza. What kind of sports do you play? How is your vegetable garden going? When is your birthday and do you have big birthday parties? I like to draw pictures and make art. I live in Marina Del Rey. And I met a stingray and I saw twenty-three seals by the dock on the water bus. I am a girl. My friend Katie is a tomboy.

I like riding a two-wheel bike and princesses and pirates and kids younger than me. I am six and a half and I have pet walking sticks and they eat rose leaves. For their birthday I gave them a drinking fountain. I have a bunk bed. I also like soccer and TV. I crawled when I was a baby.

Sincerely,
Ysabelle Ginahafe, age 6
Los Angeles

"Please send money. I love princesses."

Dear Michelle,

You are so healthy. You are the president's wife that wants everybody to get along by not fighting. Please send money. I love princesses.

Love,

Alyssa Lopez, age 7
Los Angeles

Mildred Dzib, age 10, San Francisco

Dear Mrs. Obama,

If I was to get invited to eat dinner with you I'd have so much fun. What if I was your daughter? I'd love you a whole lot and I would always play with you. Malia and Sasha are beautiful children and are so sweet to other people that they see. I would like to become friends with your two daughters. Can I? You should take Sasha and Malia to the Brooklyn Park out on 6th Street. It has a slide that goes eight feet out in the sky and it swirls all around until you get to the bottom. It has a swing that pushes by itself and if you say high it will go high, if you say low it will go low.

The Brooklyn Park closes at midnight and I stay until 10:00. It's fun. I have too much fun. When I run I burn off energy. I know that you want kids to exercise every day for an hour, but I exercise for two hours and thirty minutes every day.

Mrs. Obama, you are a great mom and I think you make a great team getting people to get along with others, so they can make more friends. I think it's great to do those great things every day.

Sincerely,
NéShawn Belt, age 7
Washington, DC

"What is bodyguards? I do not have bodyguards."

Dear Mrs. Obama and Bo,

What do you and Bo do every day? My mom does not like dogs. How old is Bo? My sister made a project about your family. How many rooms do you have? I have seven rooms. What is bodyguards? I do not have bodyguards.

Yours truly,
Axel Ortega, age 7
Chicago

"A smelly foot should be a foot that has a nose on it. Do you have a nose on your foot?"

Dear Michelle Obama,

I am Isayas, and I wanted to tell you that English is a good language because it's easier to learn. And I want to ask you — why do people make up weird names like hot dog or runny nose, or even smelly feet? Because a hot dog should be a dog that's hot and a runny nose should be a nose running, and a smelly foot should be a foot that has a nose on it. Do you get these? And do you have a nose on your foot?

Here are some jokes: What is a hissing cockroach's favorite subject in school? Hissssssssstory. What should you do to a blue elephant? Cheer it up! Why do brooms and vacuum cleaners think people are mean? Because they keep on pushing them. So, were they funny? Great!

Sincerely yours,
Isayas Bikila, age 9
Seattle

Dear Michelle Obama,

I am Belinda Garcia and I go to Gabriella Charter School and I am eleven years old. How are you and do you like living in the White House and do you have an Easy-Bake Oven? I have one right now. What I want you to do for me is to tell people to stop wasting water and I would like your family to come here. I would like you to keep the state clean. I would like you to come to every state. I would like to tell you that you are a very beautiful person.

Sincerely,
Belinda Garcia, age 11
Los Angeles

Dear Michelle Obama,

What did you cook on your Easy-Bake Oven? Have you cooked anything in the White House? Is it fun to live in the White House?

Brian Romero, age 11
Los Angeles

"Try to keep drugs off the streets. Robots may be able to help you."

Dear Michelle Obama,

Hi, our names are Nicolas and Aidan, and we are ten and nine years old. We live in Boston. We hope you send letters back to us.

I think that you should shut down cigarette and liquor companies and try to keep drugs off the streets. Robots may be able to help you. We all appreciate your hard work to make America better.

Sincerely,
Aidan Sheill-Loomis, age 9, and
Nicolas W. Brooke, age 10
Boston

"My aunt has a big house like yours, but she doesn't have a bowling alley."

Dear Mrs. Obama,

Hi, my name is Desani. I'm in the fourth grade. I'm originally from New York City. I'm rich, but I live in a small house. My aunt has a big house like yours, but she doesn't have a bowling alley.

What do you like most about living in the White House?

What I like is the bowling alley (I think you have one), playground, and theater. What I love about you is you're smart and you have a sense of humor.

Sincerely,
Desani Grant, age 8
Washington, DC

Dear Michelle Obama,

Make school lunch better because child obesity is very
bad. It's kind of the parents' fault because they listen to
their children when they ask for food and they take
vehicle transportation and don't walk or use a bike.
I think that you should continue stopping child obesity.

> Sincerely,
> *Darious Serrano,* age 11
> New York

Dear Mrs. Obama,

I'm a girl scout. I sold about 350 cookies and that's how we got patches. My Uncle Brent was in the same class as you at Whitney Young and my dad went to Whitney Young. When is your birthday? My birthday is March 30. I was born on March 30, 2003. I wrote this August 4, 2010. I bet you're happy to be the first lady.

Madison Grant, age 7
Chicago

"I mostly like to paint with my favorite color, teal. I am sure you have seen that color because it is around a lot."

Dear Michelle Obama,

I am going to tell you about what I want to be when I grow up.
But first I will tell you a little bit of myself. My name is Kelly
Tuxpan. I'm nine years old. My favorite sport is soccer and
my favorite color is teal, which is a mix of green and blue.
Okay, now what I want to be is an artist. I love to color, draw,
and paint. It is so fun. Do you like to draw? I spend most of
my time drawing, coloring, and painting. I mostly like to paint
with my favorite color, teal. I am sure you have seen that
color because it is around a lot. I hope someday I can grow
up and become a famous artist.

Sincerely,
Kelly Tuxpan, age 9
Los Angeles

Dear Mrs. OBAMA,

you are the Best LaDy
in the world if you wont to
come over you can bereeing
your Daughters and the President
if you come over i will cook you
corn, rice, Berocli, chiken, and cake.

Love, Saudia Campbell, 6

Saudia Campbell, age 6, Washington, DC

Dear Michelle Obama,

My mom always calls me Recycle Girl because I want to help the world. Please, make sure that people recycle bottles and paper.

Andrea Ramirez, age 7
Los Angeles

"Who made up the whales?"

Dear Michelle Obama,

You should clean the ocean with the oil. Who made up
the whales? Does Obama play video games? Can you give
me the new game of *Pokémon Black and White*? Can you
give me a ten-pack of $100? Can you let me live with you?

Sincerely,
Suivel Martinez, age 9
Los Angeles

Dear First Lady,

Hi! I'm Renea and I go to Greenwood Elementary in Seattle.
I think you should encourage people to stop global warming
by riding their bikes, turning off the lights, and using less
fossil fuels.

I also think that you should help homeless people by putting up
more homeless shelters. Most people that are homeless in Seattle
are wet and cold because of all the rain. I hope that you and
President Obama will consider my ideas.

Sincerely,
Renea Harris-Peterson, age 10
Seattle

Dear Michelle,

Our names are Aisha and Sumaya. We are cousins. We are
both eight years old and we go to Joyce Kilmer and Nathan
Hale Elementary School. We are writing this letter to you
because we want you to help the community.

We want you to help the old people. We want the old people
to go to hospitals and not pay for it because they don't have
a lot of money and they are sick.

In the schools we want you to help to prevent bullies. We
should have more school supplies. Also, we want the bath-
rooms to be fixed because the conditions are pretty bad.

We would be very happy if you would read our letter and do
something about it.

Sincerely,
Sumaya Ismail, age 8, and
Aisha Mahamud, age 8
Boston

"I broke my arm.
I jumped off of
a window. I got
better. I went to the
doctor and they put
a cast on me.
It was so itchy."

Dear Mrs. Obama,

Hi. My name is Samsam. I am six years old and I live in Roxbury. I am in first grade at the Nathan Hale School. My favorite pet is a cat, but I don't have one. When I was a baby, I broke my arm. I jumped off of a window. I got better. I went to the doctor and they put a cast on me. It was so itchy.

I wonder how you could stop the war. A lot of people are getting killed. If a lot of people get killed, there will be no more people in some countries. Instead of fighting wars, we could be peaceful together and be nice instead of selfish. I don't know how we'll stop the war, but I want your help.

Sincerely,
Samsam Ismail, age 6
Boston

"I am ordinary. You are the wife of President Obama."

Dear Michelle Obama,

Hello. I am Luis. You are the best wife of a president. I am ordinary. You are the wife of President Obama.

I have one question for you: You're having more babies? You have one dog. I like dogs. Okay, bye.

Sincerely,
Luis Palomar, age 11
Los Angeles

Soham Naik, age 11, Ann Arbor, Michigan

Hello Michelle Obama,

I hope that you succeed in turning the world green. I'm an eleven-year-old kid that goes to Martin Luther King School in Ann Arbor, Michigan.

I really like to read books that are realistic fiction and fiction like *Harry Potter, Artemis Fowl, Warriors,* and *Percy Jackson.* I really like how you try to get kids to learn. I really like to do math and reading. You know how you do green things? I do, too! I compost and I recycle bottles made out of aluminum and plastic.

Thank you very much and have a great fall.

Sincerely,
Soham Naik, age 11
Ann Arbor, Michigan

Dear Michelle Obama,

My name is Samantha Cho and I am nine years old. I go
to Thurston Elementary School and I am in fourth grade.
I live with my mom and dad and with my three younger
siblings named Nicholas, Nathalie, and Caitlin. Since I am
the oldest I have more responsibilities. For example, I get to
stay up later than everyone else. What do you like to do
outside? I like to play field hockey, and even though I am
not very good, I play soccer with Nicholas.

I heard you have a dog. I have a dog, too. Her name is Maggie.
I used to have two other dogs named Rosie and Max, but Max
died and Rosie had serious bathroom drama and we had to
return her. Maggie likes to run around and play with tennis
balls and bones. What does your dog like to eat? Maggie likes
to eat peanut butter, dog food, and biscuits.

What sports do you play? I play field hockey, tennis,
swimming, golf, a little bit of soccer, and I like dribbling
my basketball in the driveway. I have a field hockey game
tomorrow, and my team's name is Phoenix. I have no clue
who we will be playing, but I know I will have fun.

I live in Ypsilanti, Michigan. I really like living here. It is very fun. I like the way the climate is, even though it can get very hot and very cold! We are entering the cold stage of the year and believe me, it isn't very pretty. The leaves are beginning to fall off the trees and it is almost time to jump into a pile of leaves.

I have never seen the Great Lakes before, but from what I've heard, they sound amazing.

I hope you can pay a visit here, and if you can, maybe you can see my house. Sometimes I don't feel challenged enough in class. Maybe you can pay a visit to my school and see if you approve of the work.

Sincerely,
Samantha Cho, age 9
Ypsilanti, Michigan

D'aira Roberts, age 10, Washington, DC

Dear Michelle Obama,

What is President Obama going to change? Can you lower the gas prices? I live in Venice. You deserve to be the president's wife.

Love,

Sam Clay-Lund, age 10
Los Angeles

"What do you feed Bo? I have a dog, too. I feed him... uh, I forgot."

Dear Obama family,

Do you like basketball? What are you mostly allergic to? What do you mostly do all day? How do you feel leading the country? What would you do on a day off? What are the bodyguards' names? What do you feed Bo? I have a dog, too. I feed him… uh, I forgot. My dog is a Maltese. His name is Codey.

Your friend Alex from Chicago,
Alexander Henderson, age 8
Chicago

"Please help to stop bullying so the kids can be safe in school. Could you please do me that favor?"

Dear Mrs. Obama,

Hi, my name is Derrick. I'm nine years old. I live in Boston, Massachusetts. I'm writing to you because I would like you to talk to schools to see what they can do to stop bullying. This is really important to me because I think people can get hurt in school when there is bullying involved. I think that if you talk to schools about what kind of new rules they can come up with about bullying, this could help a lot. I really don't like the way other kids are being treated. This year, I'm going to the Paul A. Dever School in Roxbury, Massachusetts. I like that they don't let people fight and they are quick to call the cops if people are fighting. I feel safe at that school.

One idea that I would like to share with you is to talk to kids on TV and tell them how bad bullying is and what bullying can cause if it doesn't stop. So please help to stop bullying so the kids can be safe in school. Could you please do me that favor?

Sincerely,
Derrick Perez, age 9
Boston

Dear Mrs. OBama!

Erica Phillips 7

I will come to visit   the
white House for dinner.

chicken, eggs, frenchfrie

are my favorite foods.

Whut are your favorite foods?

Erica Phillips, age 7, Seattle

Dear First Lady,

Have you ever been to Las Vegas? Well I haven't, but I would love to. I heard it is fantastic and the lights are great at nighttime. There are lots of cool things you could do there like fun, scary rides. You should go there. Thanks for spending your time to read my letter. In addition, I know you are the busiest first lady and you took your time to read my letter.

Sincerely,
Natty Solomon, age 13
Seattle

"Have you ever met Justin Bieber or Jaden Smith?"

Dear First Lady,

Hi! My name is Thalia Flores. I'm from Puerto Rico and Washington, DC. Do you have fun with your daughters? Do you really have a bowling alley? Is Bo a puppy? I have a dog in Puerto Rico and her name means blonde in Spanish. Did you go to Puerto Rico before? Have you ever met Justin Bieber or Jaden Smith? Did you meet George Bush before? Well, this is the end. I hope you write me back. Bye!

Love,
Thalia Flores, age 9
Washington, DC

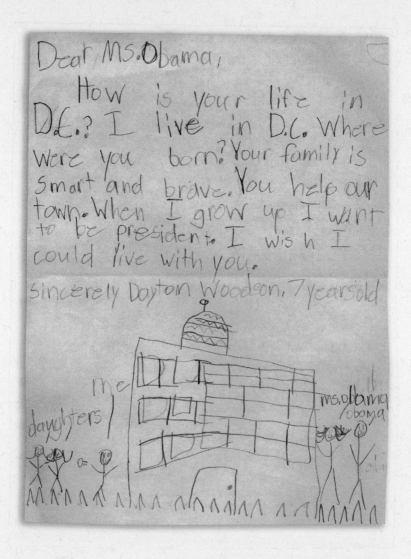

Dear Ms. Obama,

How is your life in D.C.? I live in D.C. Where were you born? Your family is smart and brave. You help our town. When I grow up I want to be president. I wish I could live with you.

Sincerely Dayton Woodson, 7 years old

Dayton Woodson, age 7, Washington, DC

Dear Michelle Obama,

It is very cool that you live in the White House. I know if I lived in the White House I would have looked in all the rooms they have because it is a very, very big house with a lot of history behind it. I am very curious about where all of the other presidents used to live. I also have a vegetable garden mixed with a little bit of flowers such as tulips, sunflowers, and roses.

Sincerely,
Veronica Ramirez, age 12
Los Angeles

iguana Dragin

Eric Butler, age 7, Washington, DC

Dear Mrs. Obama,

My favorite places are Dave and Buster's, Chuck E. Cheese, the computer lab, and GameStop. Mrs. Obama, is it true that your daughter is as big as you? I am an artist and I hope you enjoy my picture of an iguanaDragin.

Your friend,
Eric Butler, age 7
Washington, DC

Dear Michelle Obama,

My name is Ivette Paz. I live in Los Angeles and go to a charter school. The main topic on everyone's minds these days is the slower economy. Creating jobs and making sure programs have enough money can be hard. One way is to make jobs for teachers who are being laid off. Teachers are an important part of our society and are treated very unfairly. They should get more money than a hotel manager.

Sincerely,
Ivette Paz, age 12
Los Angeles

Dear Mrs. Obama,

I wanted to say you are a very good first lady — caring about kids' education and exercise. You are a very good role model to many people, including me! I think you are a very good mom. My mom agrees with me, too, I'm sure. Also I think you are brave for going to countries and giving speeches.
I also really like your Portuguese water dog, Bo. My friend said you guys call him "Bobama!" I think that's pretty cute. Do you have a nickname? If so, what is your nickname?

Sincerely,
Bianca Varlesi, age 9
Chicago

Mrs. O

Kendra Lowery, age 7, Washington, DC

Dear Mrs. Obama,

I love you. You're my favorite first lady. I like the way you share love around the world.

Your friend,

Kendra Lowery, age 7
Washington, DC

"You are eating 100% healthy. Can you put my dad in a job?"

Dear Michelle,

You are eating 100% healthy. Can you put my dad in a job? You're doing a good job helping the homeless. I'm eating healthy. I'm eating watermelon, melon, mango, and persimmons. I just want to have $200. And you have a very nice house. All I know is one of the rooms is a speech room.

> **Santos Lopez,** age 8
> Los Angeles

Dear First Lady,

Could you tell Obama to stop the war because people are dying
and give paper to the people that do not have paper? Also my
dad works for the city. Can you give him more money? His
name is Manuel and he is in the airport. And how many rooms
are there in the White House? I live in 4142. The manager
does not let us have a dog and people that live there have a dog.
Could you tell the manager we've got to have our dog back?
Thank you.

Love,
Oscar Castro, age 9
Los Angeles

Dear Mrs. Obama,

My name is Yasmeen Logan and I am twelve years old.
I live in Boston, Massachusetts. I have a little brother
named Naeem.

I am writing this letter because I think that everyone who
gets good grades should be able to get a laptop. Most kids
need laptops for school and cannot afford it like me. I need
a laptop for homework and for typing papers. I know laptops
are becoming cheaper, but they are still unaffordable for kids
like me. I think you can help us by donating some money so
we can get laptops.

I think computer companies need to give away free laptops.
I hope after reading this letter you will donate laptops.

Yours Truly,
Yasmeen Logan, age 12
Boston

Dear First Lady,

I am very vexed and sad about animal rights. Some cruel people abuse them or throw them away, and lots of animals are close to being extinct. When I think of how they feel, I cry for their suffering. Instead of complaining I decided to write ideas.

My name is Jinhee Jung and I'm eleven. I became concerned when my grandparents and I watched a movie about animal abuse. Also, my friends and I went to the library to learn more about marine biology and found lots of endangered animals, like sharks. Both of those things got me interested.

For starters, let's not hunt endangered animals. If we hunt these animals, they'll be extinct before we know all the information about them. I know that saying that we should all be vegetarians is too much, so how about we could just eat basic meats like cows, pigs, chicken, and turkeys? That would help more animals.

Sincerely,
Jinhee Jung, age 11
Seattle

Dear Michelle,

I suggest you should keep on fighting obesity. You should give your kids some freedom so they won't get stressed out. Living in the USA has brought me good moments. In Los Angeles there is a lot of danger because there are so many gangs. The thing I would like the least about living in the White House is that you could get attacked. The things I would like most about living in the White House is how it looks and how it is a mansion. If I had these 10 minutes with you, I would talk to you about my experiences living in the USA.

Sincerely,
Javier Vaca, age 12
Los Angeles

"Do what you can
and it'll
be perfect."

Dear Michelle,

My name is Laurea. I go to Pattengill Elementary. The playground is awesome there. I love to hang out on the swings. Do what you can and it'll be perfect. My favorite game is Apples to Apples. Wouldn't it be awesome if pickles grew on trees?

From,
Laurea Wright, age 8
Ann Arbor, Michigan

Dear First Lady,

My name is Katherine Proulx. I am going to be a sixth-grader at Seattle Girls' School. This year at school we learned all about environmental stewardship. We went on tons of field trips and we learned a lot about the world.

Did you know that only one percent of recyclable plastic water bottles actually *get* recycled? It's true. And the rest either get put in landfills across the country to stay for thousands of years or get burned in incinerators that emit toxic chemicals.

I think that plastic water bottles should be banned from the White House and all White House events. Just doing that could really make a big difference!

P.S. I *love* your clothes!

P.P.S. And your dog is so cute!

Sincerely,
Katherine Logan Proulx, age 12
Seattle

Dear Michelle Obama,

One of the solutions to greenhouse gas is hydrogen fusion. It's when you fuse four Hs and you make an HE and that releases a tremendous amount of heat. And after boiling the water and making electricity, it turns out that it makes, I think, ten times the amount of electricity it takes to create the heat. The only problem with this is that it makes enough electricity to charge all the houses on a street for a couple weeks, but while traveling through the power lines two-thirds of the electricity is lost by the time it reaches the house. So it will be good to invest money in the power lines problem. Also, one of the best forms of renewable energy is solar panels. Even though they're expensive now, I suggest investing money in commercials for them. The more they sell the cheaper they get.

Omid Tavakoli, age 12
Flint, Michigan

Dear First Lady Michelle Obama,

What are your plans for the White House vegetable
garden? I think your family should eat the vegetables.
My favorite vegetables are carrots and green beans.
Do you grow those at the White House?

Love,
Kennedy Clay-Lund, age 5
Los Angeles

Dear Mrs. Obama,

My name is Arezu. I am nine years old. I turned nine on September 30 and I got a little Hexbug Nano. I really want to meet your daughters, especially Sasha. When did she turn nine? I was going to Washington, DC, but ended up in Virginia. I did go to the Smithsonian. Anyways, please send a letter back. (Oh and can Sasha send a letter?)

Best wishes,
Arezu Tavakoli, age 9
Flint, Michigan

Dear Ms.
ObAMA,
I love
Your dog.

Earl Harris, age 8, Boston

Dear Mrs. Obama,

Is it embarrassing doing a speech? Do you have to practice?
I have to practice playing my violin. I have to do recitals.
Is it fun leading the country? If I were the president, I would
give the poor people all of my money.

P.S. I do not like money, except quarters.

From,
Will Garrett, age 7
Chicago

Dear Michelle Obama,

Can we recycle more? Did you know that every twenty minutes a bird dies? My teacher Ms. Bhatt taught me that. Can you send me this: the new Pokémon game named *Pokémon Black and White*. Please. I'm twelve years old and I drink *café*. My school name is Grandview Elementary School.

Sincerely,
Izequiel Martinez, age 12
Los Angeles

Dear Mrs. Obama,

My name is Grace. I'm in fourth grade and I'm nine years old.
I do Girls on the Run. I also do soccer. I think it's cool that
you're doing the "Let's Move" campaign. In April I broke my
arm. I had surgery and they put pins in, but they didn't hurt
at all when they came out. One time when I was going to the
bathroom I didn't know the toilet seat was up. I fell in a little.
It was gross. Oh! What are you doing on Halloween?

Love,
Grace Vowels, age 8
Ann Arbor, Michigan

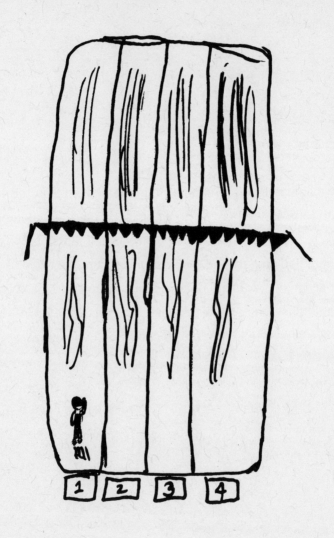

Mara Connell, age 12, Seattle

Dear First Lady,

My name is Mara Connell, I am twelve years old, and have a passion for basketball and swimming. Although in this letter I am writing about swimming.

All around the country there are public pools that are closing because they can't afford to be open — even in the hotter places like Arizona. Swimming doesn't only bring joy to kids of all ages, but it's also a form of exercise. Whether it's just playing, going for a lap swim, or swimming lessons, it's a lot better than sitting around and watching TV.

As you can see, this topic is very important to me! I love swimming and the last thing I want is to see my local public pool close down. So to make sure that doesn't happen, I want to raise money for the public pools in the U.S. If this problem means anything to you, I would like for your help to open back up some of these pools. Thank you for your help and for reading this letter.

Sincerely,
Mara Connell, age 12
Seattle

"I put my hand in the toilet, in the toilet water and grabbed the flosser! It was really gross! Why are there flossers in the bathroom anyway!?"

Dear Michelle Obama,

Hello, my name is Anna Rinvelt. I go to Wines Elementary.
I'm eight years old. I really like art. One time I saw a flosser
in the toilet. I tried to get it out with toilet paper, but it sank
to the bottom. So I put my hand in the toilet, in the toilet
water and grabbed the flosser! It was really gross! Why are
there flossers in the bathroom anyway!?

Love,
Anna Rinvelt, age 8
Ann Arbor, Michigan

"Please bring me scary stories like the ones my teacher has. For example, a book full of scary stories that are very, very scary."

Dear Michelle Obama,

My name is Juan. I have two younger sisters, Michelle and Rachelle. Make the world better. Please bring me scary stories like the ones my teacher has. For example, a book full of scary stories that are very, very scary. Bring me a thing to put my books in because I have a lot of books and they are too heavy in my backpack. Please bring me a cute fish, too, like the ones in *Finding Nemo* — the movie.

I want to be a teacher when I grow up because I want to teach other kids things they like learning, like how to take a test. When I am at school and it is recess time I like to play with my friends. My favorite colors are blue, brown, and yellow. Next year I will be going to the third grade. In the third grade I am going to learn very fast because I will practice the tests very fast, but sometimes I get some answers wrong. I know I can do better than that. My favorite food to eat is pepperoni pizza because it tastes very, very, very, very good and smells yummy.

Thank you,
Juan Benitez, age 7
San Francisco

Hello Michelle Obama,

Tell Barack I say hi. I would give you advice: don't go to too many meetings. My advice to your family is to not think negative too much. My life in Los Angeles is good because it does not snow. The White House is good to live in because it is big.

Matthew Jordan, age 11
Los Angeles

Dear Michelle Obama,

Hi. I'm Evan Maley. I am eight and a half. You should come to Michigan to see the Great Lakes in the winter and summer. You should come to a Michigan football game. The stadium is really cool! If you come, I hope they will win. It would make me happy. I hope you are doing good stuff for the United States, and the Army. Every once in a while I get the neighborhood to play football. I love to play outside. I hope the whole United States gets really active and stops playing so many video games. Then America would be even better. Do you have a lot of Silly Bandz? I do. Do your daughters play sports? I play lacrosse. I hope you still do good stuff for America.

Go Blue!

Sincerely,
Evan Maley, age 8
Ann Arbor, Michigan

"P.S. My Auntie Cheryl thinks you should have another kid, but only if you want."

Dear First Lady,

I would like to make a few suggestions about school lunches and how they should be checked out before sending the lunches into schools. For example, one day it was sticky macaroni and cheese day at school and one kid dropped his plate and the macaroni and cheese flew up in the air and bounced into his hands! Wow, that was really disgusting! Anyways, that's one reason you should at least consider, Mrs. Obama, that we have to make sure that our children have healthy lunches with more fruits and veggies.

We should also consider challenging students more in classes so they know that we expect them to do their best and no less. Thank you for listening.

P.S. My Auntie Cheryl thinks you should have another kid, but only if you want.

Sincerely,

Segan Araya, age 12
Seattle

Dear Mrs. Obama,

My name is Terry Wu. I am ten years old. My favorite subjects are science and math. I have no brothers or sisters. My favorite songs are "Vanilla Twilight," "Hey, Soul Sister," "Big Time Rush," "A Million Fireflies," and "Rainbow Wing." My favorite instruments are piano and guitar.

My name is Nelson Olawoyin. I am eleven years old. My favorite subjects are math and science. I have one brother named Aaron. My dad adores both of you. I play three instruments: violin, recorder, and piano. My favorite songs are "Young Forever," "Don't Stop Believing," and "Heartbreaker."

Our major issue is the war that is going on. We know that a lot of people are being killed during this war. We also know that you are trying your best to stop it. We think that you should strengthen the Afghan military so they can defend themselves against Al Qaeda.

Sincerely yours,
Terry Wu, age 10, and
Nelson Olawoyin, age 11
Boston

Dear Michelle,

My name is Sebastian and I did a report on you. I am in the eighth grade. I learned that you were raised on the South Side of Chicago and also that you visit schoolkids to help them study. I am tall and I like to sleep a lot, but some days I wake up early.

Sincerely,
Sebastian Martinez, age 13
Brooklyn

"Please put a statue of me in Echo Park... JK. No, really. I want a tuxedo on the statue."

Dear Michelle Obama,

I think your husband should legalize immigration. Please put
a statue of me in Echo Park. Thank you. JK. No, really.
I want a tuxedo on the statue.

Love,
Andres Ortega, age 11
Los Angeles

"I have a pet.
His name is Bird.
He is a rabbit.
I know it's
confusing."

Dear Michelle Obama,

I go to school at Grand View. I hate the cafeteria food.
It is so disgusting. I have a pet. His name is Bird. He is
a rabbit. I know it's confusing.

Sincerely,
Jesus Ruiz, age 10
Los Angeles

Dear Michelle Obama,

My name is Ishani and I go to Carpenter Elementary. I don't use a school bus. I know how to whistle. Michigan is a cool state. Its state bird is an American robin and it is the state of the Great Lakes. In the winter the waves freeze and it looks cool. I saw the White House during summer break.

Sincerely,
Ishani Gaidhane, age 9
Ann Arbor, Michigan

Dear Michelle,

Can you help my family? We're about to lose our house. Make the world a better place. What is your favorite food?

Sincerely,
Jesenia Reza, age 9
Los Angeles

"Do you have a turtle? I have a turtle. My turtle's name is Slurpie. I had two, but one died. His name was Churro."

Dear Michelle Obama,

Do you wear glasses? Do you have a MySpace? I like the computer. Do you have a turtle? I have a turtle. My turtle's name is Slurpie. I had two, but one died. His name was Churro. Have you ever been to the Staples Center? Have you ever bungee jumped? I haven't. I want to go. Have you ever gone to outer space?

Sincerely,
Robert Rodriguez, age 12
Los Angeles

Dear Ms. Obama,

Hello Michelle Obama. What is the recipe for Barack's chili? I need to try it. Los Angeles is awesome. All it needs is a football team. The Dodgers are awesome, too. Do you eat a bacon burger for breakfast? I do.

Jason Lee, age 11
Los Angeles

Dear Michelle Obama,

My name is Jerry and I am very excited to be writing a letter to you. I would like to ask you some questions and tell you things about me. Do you like your vegetable garden? I like fruit, eggs, and bacon. My favorite breakfast is cereal and bananas. We would really like to taste Mr. Barack Obama's chili and your linguine — it sounds delicious. Did you like being a kid when you were little? I really like being a kid. It was a pleasure writing you a letter, Mrs. Obama.

Sincerely,
Jerry Barrales, age 12
Los Angeles

"Tigers are one of the animals I like. They are getting hunted down for clothes and furniture!"

Dear First Lady,

What's your favorite animal? I have lots of animals that I like.

Tigers are one of the animals I like. They are getting hunted down for clothes and furniture! There are fewer tigers each year! You can start a new fashion trend that doesn't involve animals. Like using cotton, silk, etc.

What would you do if your favorite animal was being hunted?

Sincerely,
Meron Solomon, age 10
Seattle

Dear Mrs. Obama,

If I were invited to your house for dinner, with Sasha and
Malia, I would want to eat chicken nuggets with French fries.
Also for dessert I would want an ice cream sundae with choco-
late syrup, whipped cream, sprinkles, and a cherry on top.
I want to meet you very much and visit the White House.

Your friend,
Melvin Holloway III, age 7
Washington, DC

Dear Mrs. Obama,

You make great speeches. You are such a great person.
I saw some of your videos on a computer. I really like those
videos. When I saw you in one of the videos I laughed when
I saw you dancing.

Love,
Destiny Morales, age 6
Los Angeles

Dear Michelle Obama,

My name is Zavier Williams. I am nine years old and going into the fourth grade at Joseph Lee Academy. I am in an advanced work class. My favorite subject is math.

I have a couple questions that I would like to ask. Could you please give the homeless people food, clothes, and a place to live? And please tell the people to stop littering because it is hurting the planet.

Could you come up to Boston to visit the schools to see what the children need? In my school we need more gym classes for exercise. Also, what is your favorite animal? My favorite animals are zebras, parrots, and tarantulas.

Sincerely,
Zavier Williams, age 9
Boston

Dear Michelle Obama,

Could you change the USA by caring for other people and violence? One more thing, how about the people that don't have a home or the people that don't have food? Could you make all the schools have time to play more soccer?

Josue Juarez, age 6
Los Angeles

Dear Michelle Obama,

Our names are Maya and Alia. We go to Delphi Academy in Milton, Massachusetts.

Our problem is the oil spill in the Gulf of Mexico. What we know about it is that animals are dying. The animals can't see so they can't get food because they're stuck in the oil. We think more people should help with cleaning up the oil in the Gulf of Mexico. We think people should be in teams for different areas of the Gulf to help clean it up. We also think that we should get more people to clean the animals and we think that you should clean up part of the Gulf so that the animals can swim in the clean part while the other part is getting cleaned up.

Sincerely,
Maya Joseph-Lacet, age 8,
and *Alia Abdul-Jabbaar,* age 9
Boston

Dear Mrs. Obama,

Thank you for helping the president — for helping him with his campaigning and by helping him do speeches. Thank you for helping people in need and supporting them and sticking up for them. I hope you are happy living in the White House. Thank you for helping kids get active with LeBron James. I hope your family will get elected for a second term. Can you ask the president to make animal shelters stop killing animals? And try to help kids get an early start in reading.

Neyin Sanders, age 9
Chicago

DON'T GO TO THE
BATHROOM IN THE YARD

Kids' Letters to Sasha, Malia, and Bo Obama

"P.S. I'm not trying to stalk your dog."

Dear Bo,

You are so cute. You are the cutest dog in the world. I just
want to kiss your little doggie cheeks and give you a hug.
They are so lucky to have you as their dog. I wish I had a dog
like you, instead I am stuck with cats. :(

You are so cool. Bye. :)

P.S. I'm not trying to stalk your dog. He's just soooooo cute!

Your friend,
Sarih Anderson, age 11
Washington, DC

"Don't tell anybody that my parents were married at the same place your parents were married!"

Dear Sasha,

My name is Sabrina. I live near your Chicago home in Hyde Park. Me and my brother's preschool is across the street. I have met Suhala (your cousin). What rooms can't you use? Do you have allergies? I have allergies to pollen. What is the silliest thing Bo has done? What is the biggest room in the White House? How many teeth have you lost? I have lost six. What are your favorite chapter books? I like *Judy Moody* and a lot of others. Don't tell anybody that my parents were married at the same place your parents were married! I want to be famous like you. Do you know how to play chess? I do. I have an organic garden, too. I hope you are okay. I'm going to end my message. Bye!

Your friend in Chicago,
Sabrina Ricer-Wurr, age 7
Chicago

Dear Malia and Sasha,

My name is Camila and I like gum and spaghetti. My favorite subject is science. What is your favorite color? My favorite colors are red and purple. My house color is purple. I color and cut paper. When I grow up I want to be a fashion designer. My favorite dish at home is pizza. I wish I could do fireworks.

Love,
Camila Gomez, age 6
San Francisco

Dear Sasha,

The name of my school is South Loop. Is Malia annoying? I have a brother and he is very annoying. How is it being the president's daughter? Do you get to go on a lot of trips? Do you get to see your dad a lot? He must be very busy. Do you feed Bo? Do you take him on walks? Do you have your own room? I have my own room. It has two beds. How big is your dad's office? How big is your room? What does your dad do to rule the country? Is he very busy and tired? How many bodyguards do you have?

From your friend,
Teagan Elizabeth Bigger, age 7
Chicago

Dear Obama Family,

What is up? This is Kelsi A. Gross. I love your work! I like
dancing. Have you traveled a lot of places? If so and you go
on another trip, TAKE ME WITH YOU! Oh… let me tell
you a little bit about myself. My favorite singer is Beyoncé
Knowles. I like the color blue and my favorite dessert is
banana pudding!

Your friend,
Kelsi A. Gross, age 11
Washington, DC

Dear Sasha,

I love to cook cake. What is it like to live in the White Home?
And what is your favorite color? What is your mom's favorite
color? And you are so cute and Obama is a very good
president. How old are you, Sasha? And what is your sister's
favorite color? And you are famous.

Do you like the White Home? What is your favorite game in
the White Home? Does your mom pick your games in the
White Home?

Yovana Sanchez, age 8
San Francisco

"Well, I think you're lucky because you get almost everything you want."

Dear Sasha and Malia Obama,

Hello, my name is Amy Ramirez. I am ten. I live in San Francisco. Is it true you have your own private bowling alley? If my dad was president of the United States, I would be proud. Well, I think you're lucky because you get almost everything you want.

Sincerely,
Amy Ramirez, age 10
San Francisco

Dear Bo are You hungry?

Ofeiba Allen-Harding, age 6, Boston

Dear Obama Family,

My name is Donovan McCoy. I have some advice for you
guys. First, my advice for Mr. Obama. You might know
the government. Please, do everything in your power to
help it. Mrs. Obama, please help your husband out. Sasha
and Malia, stay in school and get the best education for
you. And last, but not least, Bo. *Please*, Bo, don't go to the
bathroom in the yard.

From,
Donovan McCoy, age 10
Washington, DC

Dear Sasha,

You are very pretty and smart. I hope you had a nice summer.
Do you like living in the White House? I'm going to turn
nine in March.

From,
Tracy Novas, age 8 1/2
Brooklyn

Dear Malia,

Tell your dad and your mom to come visit my house to come play with me. And you and your sister can come, too. We can eat something, walk around Brooklyn. I live on 9th Street. Maybe you should come next week. Please?

Bye!
Catherine Taveras, age 9
Brooklyn

Dear Malia and Sasha,

My name is Oceano. I am nine years old. My favorite colors are black and blue and purple. Can you cross your eyes? What's your favorite candy? What do you like to do when you are not studying? I like to draw and I don't like to use colored pencils. If I went to the White House to visit you, I would like to play *LittleBigPlanet* and ping-pong. Is it weird being the daughters of the president? Does he take you out for doughnuts? What time is it in Washington, DC right now? Do you wear fancy clothes? Can you speak any other languages apart from English? I know some words in Japanese. I live in San Francisco. I like it because it is small. I used to live in Southern California. I love to play and I play a lot, and I love to write. Do you play any sports? I play ping-pong and swimming.

Sincerely,
Oceano Pettiford, age 9
San Francisco

Dear Bo,

What do you do? Do you get treats all day? I have a dog named Huckleberry. And he is a golden retriever who likes to play fetch. Huck would like to chase you.

Your awesome friend,
Brewster Hutchinson, age 5
Chicago

Dear Bo,

How does it feel to be the president's pet? I get only fish for pets. Do you get distracted when you need to be alone? I usually get distracted by my sister. Do you go on many walks? If you do, I bet if we did a race, you would win. Where do you sleep? I sleep with my sister. Does anybody guard you? I wish someone would guard me. Who gives you baths? I'm usually with my mother. Do you brush your teeth often? I have to do it twice a day. What do you do when Mr. Obama has a day off? When my dad has a day off, I usually go hiking. Do you sleep all day? I do, because I'm really lazy. One more question. Do you usually play with Sasha and Malia? I usually play with my sister. Thank you for reading this letter.

A Chicago citizen,
Rachel Tang, age 9
Chicago

Acknowledgments

Jory John, Eli Horowitz, Ryan Lewis, Eliana Stein,
Dave Eggers, Justin Carder, Chris Ying, Brian McMullen,
Adam Krefman, Sam Riley, Meagan Day, Ben Shattuck,
Jill Haberkern, Kent Green, Jorie Schuetz, Blythe Tai,
Mike Valente, Walter Green, Christine Williams, and all
of the staff, volunteers, and students from 826 centers
across the country: thank you.

San Francisco

WWW.826VALENCIA.ORG

Los Angeles

WWW.826LA.ORG

New York

WWW.826NYC.ORG

Chicago

WWW.826CHI.ORG

Ann Arbor

WWW.826MICHIGAN.ORG

Seattle

WWW.826SEATTLE.ORG

Boston

WWW.826BOSTON.ORG

Washington, DC

WWW.826DC.ORG

826 NATIONAL

826 National is a family of nonprofit organizations dedicated to helping students, ages six to eighteen, with expository and creative writing at eight locations across the country. 826 chapters are located in San Francisco, Los Angeles, New York, Chicago, Ann Arbor, Seattle, Boston, and Washington, DC.

Our mission is based on the understanding that great leaps in learning can happen with one-on-one attention, and that strong writing skills are fundamental to future success.

Each 826 chapter offers after-school tutoring, field trips, workshops, and in-school programs — all free of charge — for students, classes, and schools.

826 is especially committed to supporting teachers, offering services and resources for English-language learners, and publishing student work.

To learn more or get involved, please visit
WWW.826NATIONAL.ORG